LITTLE QUICK FIX:

WHAT KIND OF RESEARCHER ARE YOU?

Sara Miller McCune founded SAGE Publishing in 1965 to support the dissemination of usable knowledge and educate a global community. SAGE publishes more than 1000 journals and over 800 new books each year, spanning a wide range of subject areas. Our growing selection of library products includes archives, data, case studies and video. SAGE remains majority owned by our founder and after her lifetime will become owned by a charitable trust that secures the company's continued independence.

Los Angeles | London | New Delhi | Singapore | Washington DC | Melbourne

LITTLE
QUICK FIX:
WHAT KIND OF
RESEARCHER
ARE YOU?

Janet E.
Salmons

Los Angeles | London | New Delhi
Singapore | Washington DC | Melbourne

Los Angeles | London | New Delhi
Singapore | Washington DC | Melbourne

SAGE Publications Ltd
1 Oliver's Yard
55 City Road
London EC1Y 1SP

SAGE Publications Inc.
2455 Teller Road
Thousand Oaks, California 91320

SAGE Publications India Pvt Ltd
B 1/I 1 Mohan Cooperative Industrial Area
Mathura Road
New Delhi 110 044

SAGE Publications Asia-Pacific Pte Ltd
3 Church Street
#10-04 Samsung Hub
Singapore 049483

Editor: Alysha Owen
Editorial assistant: Lauren Jacobs
Production editor: Victoria Nicholas
Marketing manager: Ben Sherwood
Cover design: Shaun Mercier
Typeset by: C&M Digitals (P) Ltd, Chennai, India

Library of Congress Control Number: 2020934601

British Library Cataloguing in Publication data

A catalogue record for this book is available from
the British Library

ISBN 978-1-5297-3591-8 (pbk)

Contents

summary

Everything in
this book!

Section 1   Research integrity is about more than ethics review. **Review boards look at research designs to make sure they conform to ethical standards. Integrity is about the way we conduct our work, whether alone or with others.**

Section 2   Research is about finding answers and understanding. **Curious researchers use critical and creative thinking to keep an open mind.**

Section 3   Research makes an impact when we communicate our purpose and findings. **While researchers work within institutions, agencies, or disciplines, research that makes a difference is understood beyond usual boundaries.**

Section 4 Collaborative researchers can accomplish more together. Some research activities are independent of others, but we usually need to collaborate with a team, partners or gatekeepers, specialists, archivists, and/or co-authors.

Section 5 Researchers understand the implications of being an insider or an outsider. When we come from outside an organization, culture, or community, we need to enter with understanding and respect. When we come from outside an organization, culture, or community, we need to be aware of our own perspectives and biases.

Section 6 Researchers' intentions are challenged by schedules, institutional, supervisory, or funding requirements, sustained motivation, and other constraints. We need to cultivate mindful reflection. To stay focused, make time for self-care in order to be our best.

Section

1

Research integrity is about more than ethics review

What does it mean to be a researcher who acts with integrity?

summary

A researcher who acts with integrity is honest, trustworthy, respectful, and ethical.

Integrity is about doing the right thing at all times

Scholars and the public at large look to researchers for trustworthy answers to hard questions. For empirical research findings to counter disinformation in the Internet age, readers need to believe that researchers are honest.

Credibility is based on the reputation of science for generating truths we can rely on. We assume that researchers will approach their work ethically – even when they labour on their own, behind closed doors. Integrity-in-action means researchers will do more than simply avoid wrongdoing or questionable practices.

When we take on the role of researcher, we discover that we are being held to high standards. This means we must go beyond simply adhering to a set of guidelines. We must find our own moral compass and follow it from the first steps of design through to the final steps of reporting and disseminating results.

RESEARCH ETHICS AND THEN SOME

Researchers engage in a wide range of activities, from identifying problems and questions, designing and conducting inquiries, analysing and interpreting data, to disseminating findings. Ethical dilemmas are potentially present at every small or large step in the process.

'Research ethics' describes the responsibility of the researcher towards others, including society broadly, other scholars, and, most importantly, those whose attitudes, behaviours, and experiences we are studying. Ethical researchers commit to protect their human subjects. We need to show that we have minimized any risks, and that subjects understand the voluntary nature of their participation.

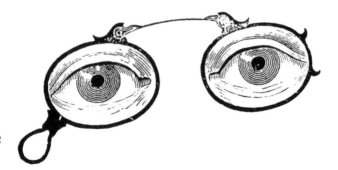

FOLLOWING PROTOCOL

Questions are different for studies that use data from archives, written or published materials, Big Data or datasets, than for those with participants. We might need to show that we have permission to access the materials, and that the materials were collected or generated in an ethical way. These issues are typically evaluated by an institutional or ethics review board at the design stage, before the study formally begins.

However, while the inquiry is underway, researchers are expected to take responsibility for their own actions and uphold high ethical standards. As students, research choices are often constrained by institutional guidelines or other parameters. Students' research work is observed or reviewed by research supervisors and committees. When we move beyond student days, ongoing ethical review is rarely part of an oversight process. Now our personal commitment to integrity is really tested.

A LASTING LESSON ABOUT CHARACTER

As a small child, a family friend tried to explain what it meant to be 'good'. She said that being good means being your best when no one is looking. It is easy to be good when others see what we're doing, and reward us with positive affirmations. But how do we act when others are out of sight? This childhood lesson seems relevant to our thinking about integrity and research because much of the work of the researcher is carried out independently. We assume that researchers will approach their work ethically – even when they labour behind closed doors.

FROM PERSONAL INTEGRITY TO PUBLIC TRUST

We assume that researchers are honest, transparent, and respectful. We expect researchers to exercise some measure of virtue ethics; that is, we expect that they will rely on an internal compass, a personal value system, or moral code when making decisions.

When researchers appropriate others' work without proper citations, misrepresent methods or findings, shade the truth or lie, the implications extend beyond individual wrongdoing. Participants can be harmed when their interview or survey answers are not respected, or when confidentiality is breached.

ACTIONS HAVE
CONSEQUENCES

More broadly, respect for scientific research at large can be damaged when false research is revealed. Bad actions, even by a few, can jeopardize future research by reducing the likelihood of funding or the credibility of well-researched policy recommendations. Other scholars in the field, practitioners, community members and families look to research for new thinking and answers. Respect for the recommendations made from empirical research depends on trust. When we commit to act with integrity, we do our part for the greater good.

INTEGRITY AND IMPACT

Today's wary public needs not only trustworthy findings, they need clear explanations of what researchers are doing, how, and why. They need us to answer two basic questions: how do I know you are telling the truth and what difference can this truth make in my life? They need to see the good ideas we discover put into practice to improve the lives of individuals and the health of the planet. To respond, we need to start with some soul-searching to make sure we are guided by respected ethical principles and norms, and with our moral compass.

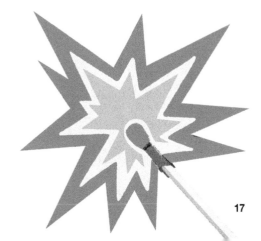

Follow these flow charts to see if you grasp the importance of integrity in doing research.

Are you ready to commit to ethical practice in the large and small steps you take as a researcher?

No

Yes

Learn and reflect!

Move on to the next question

Reflect on your values and clarify your research purpose

Talk with practising researchers in your field about the ways they act on their ethical principles

Look for readings about ethics and research ethics and think about how you would handle different situations

Are you ready to fulfil your research roles, whether you are a solo researcher or member of a research team?

No

Yes

Move on to the next chapter...

Learn and reflect!

Look for readings about the role of the researcher, including first-hand accounts or cases about conducting research

Reflect on your goals for the research project, and the strengths you bring to it

Section

Research is about finding answers and understanding

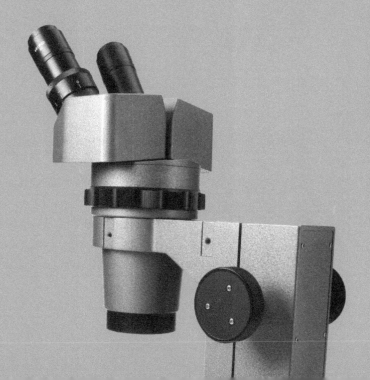

What mindsets and thinking skills do researchers need?

summary

Researchers are curious and open-minded. They use both critical and creative thinking throughout the study.

Researchers are innately curious

Researchers begin from a curious mindset to identify a problem or question. They are open-minded and accept the fact that what they expect to find might not be what is shown in the data. Researchers use critical thinking to analyse potential research problems and approaches to study them. Researchers use creative thinking for problem-solving, producing something unique, or imagining novel ways to apply findings. Researchers use both critical and creative thinking when they analyse data and present results. While most of us have patterns of thought we rely on, savvy researchers avoid ruts, and continue to develop their capacity for critical and creative thinking.

RESEARCHERS
ARE EXPLORERS

Researchers determine a destination, draw the maps, and set off on a journey. No matter how precise the planning might have been, they realize that unforeseen circumstances might mean that they don't end up in the place they intended to reach. This kind of open-mindedness is not easy. But it is a fundamental outlook that researchers must adopt. Otherwise, we use the means of research to simply confirm or affirm what we expected to find. The mode of exploration researchers use is distinctly different from that of the practitioner. Where they will try to find solutions to immediate dilemmas by looking at best practices and proven strategies, the researcher needs to dig deeper.

CRITICAL AND CREATIVE THINKING

The researcher wants to know who has studied this problem, from what ontological, epistemological, and theoretical perspectives, and using what methodology? What did they find and what did they miss? Where are the gaps in knowledge? How do those earlier studies inform the way I will approach my project?

One way to adopt a scholarly perspective is through the exercise of critical and creative thinking. These two types of thinking are complementary. At its simplest, critical thinking uses analysis. We look at an issue from multiple angles, we take it apart and evaluate the pieces. Creative thinking uses imagination. We look at different ways the issue might be interpreted or addressed and how ideas can be synthesized into a new approach. We use critical thinking to understand a problem and creative thinking to find a new resolution.

CRITICAL AND CREATIVE THINKING OVER THE COURSE OF A STUDY

Here is one way to consider intersections between critical and creative thinking over the course of a study.

Planning the study

Use critical thinking to:

- evaluate potential research problem(s) from multiple angles

- analyse the scholarly literature

- evaluate perspectives from other schools of thought or disciplines.

Use creative thinking to:

- look beyond the typical ways research problems are identified

- draw ideas from related contemporary writing, media, and social media to learn from viewpoints outside of academia.

Designing the study

Use critical thinking to:

- articulate clear, concise research questions and/or hypotheses

- evaluate and select theoretical and methodological options

- evaluate data needs and select population and collection options.

Use creative thinking to:

- invent theories or methodologies

- adapt theories or methodologies from other cultures or disciplines

- develop/adapt interview questions, observation guides, and instruments

- consider visual or creative methods for collecting data.

Conducting the study

Use critical thinking to:

- Continue to analyse and evaluate study progress and adjust as necessary.

Use creative thinking to:

- collect data from human participants in ingenious ways, so that you can gain the cooperation of gatekeepers and develop rapport conducive to questioning/surveying participants

- come up with alternative options if plans fall through

- use varied forms of communication, including visual forms, when partners or participants do not share your language or have different learning styles.

Making sense of the data

- critically analyse the data

- analyse and describe results in ways that will help readers understand the significance of the study.

- interpret the themes and trends emerging from the analysis

- visualize the data.

Sharing results

Use critical thinking to:

- analyse and describe results in ways that will help readers understand the significance of the study.

Use creative thinking to:

- discover imaginative ways to present findings and reach those who can use them. Use visuals, graphics, media, and links to related resources.

Applying the results for impact

Use critical thinking to:

- understand the needs in the field, evaluate the ways findings match needs, and take steps to apply new knowledge to real problems.

Use creative hinking to:

- imagine new ways to use what you learned from the study.

A researcher's mindset, and comfort with using different ways of thinking, is cultivated over time. Most of us start with tendencies towards either the critical, analytic way of thinking or the creative, synthesis-oriented way of thinking. However, as we grow our research capabilities, it is important to develop a wider range of ways to approach the design, conduct, and dissemination of research.

CRITICAL QUESTIONS RESEARCHERS ASK

- Who studied this problem?

- What questions were asked? What hypotheses did they try to prove?

- Were they seminal thinkers or emerging scholars?

- What worldviews were influential?

- What theories informed their inquiries?

- What methodology and methods were used?

- What population/datasets were studied?

- What was learned?

- What claims were made and supported? How?

- What are the implications for scholars?

- How can findings inform policies or practices?

CREATIVE QUESTIONS RESEARCHERS ASK

- Can I reframe this question?

- Can approaches from other disciplines be used to study this question or problem?

- What connections can I make?

- Could different methods be used to offer response modes, for example using visual methods with participants who have difficulty communicating verbally?

- Can findings be applied in other settings?

Take a moment to reflect on your own style and strengths

How do you *think?*

Do you feel that your own strengths are on the critical thinking or the creative side?

....

....

....

....

What can you do to develop a more holistic set of research skills?

....

....

....

....

How do you *act?*

This week, try using critical and creative thinking in a daily task. For example: if I chose grocery shopping as the task, I might use critical thinking to analyse the ingredients of a product. I might use creative thinking to choose a new recipe and buy food I haven't cooked before.

Now reflect on which is your natural style. How could you develop your critical or creative side?

. . . .

. . . .

. . . .

. . . .

Research makes an impact
when we communicate our
purpose and findings

Section

3

What communication skills do researchers need?

summary

Verbal and non-verbal, written and
multimedia, online and face-to-face,
one-to-one and group communication
skills are essential for researchers.

Researchers use a wide range of communication skills

We need to be able to clearly communicate the aims, purpose, and approach in order to get our studies approved or funded. We need to be able to communicate clearly with participants and with people who can allow entry to sites where we do field work or access Big Data or archives. Importantly, we need to be able to clearly communicate our findings by presenting and writing about them. Throughout these research activities we need to be careful listeners. In today's world we need to be comfortable communicating with people outside our own cultures and disciplines, using technology tools as well as interacting face-to-face. Are you confident that you have the communication skills you need to be a researcher?

CAN YOU COMMUNICATE AS A RESEARCHER?

Communication skills are essential to researchers, no matter what kind of study you are conducting. Whether you are arranging a research site, collecting data by interviewing participants, or working with librarians or archivists to access data sets or documents, you will need to communicate with a wide range of people.

Dictionary definitions of 'communication' describe the exchange between individuals through a common system of symbols, signs, or behaviour. 'Exchange' suggests that communication involves two or more people, and a two-way process. We need to convey our messages and listen to others. The next part is trickier, because it describes a 'common system of symbols, signs, or behaviour'. Sometimes we need to communicate with people who do not share our system. They might speak a different language or interpret behaviours differently. In these situations, we need to make sure we are sensitive to these differences and still managing to communicate clearly and respectfully.

POTENTIAL CHALLENGES

Here are some common challenges and tips for success:

- We need to communicate one way with scholars in our own field and another way with scholars in other fields. Within our field, we use acronyms and can expect others to understand common theories and methodologies. When we cross disciplines, we need to clarify our terms and describe approaches clearly.

- We need to communicate one way with scholars and another way with policy-makers or practitioners who might use our research. When we move outside of academia, others may be more interested in practical matters and problem-solving and less interested in theories and methods. We need to craft succinct descriptions and illustrative stories that appeal to non-academics.

- We need to communicate with research partners or participants. Research partners can include staff in agencies or institutions. Reaching research participants might require us to communicate across cultural and other boundaries. Preparation will be essential to success.

- We need to communicate electronically. We might need to adapt our electronic communication styles depending on who we are trying to reach. The text messaging, social media posts, and email we use for social or student communications may or may not be appropriate.

- We need to communicate face-to-face. We need to make eye contact and demonstrate emotional intelligence when communicating in person. We need to understand any cultural contexts that might influence whether we need to communicate more formally or include/avoid discussion of personal matters. What is rude in one culture might be polite in another!

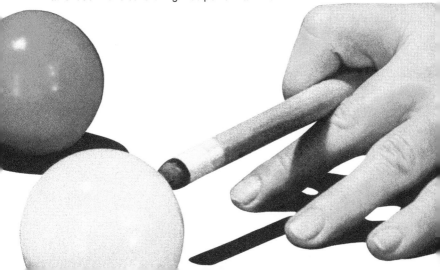

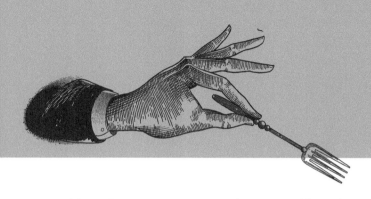

- We need to read non-verbal cues. In-person or videoconference communications are enhanced by non-verbal signals. These can include:

  - Chronemics: pacing and timing of speech and the length of silence before a response.

  - Paralinguistic communication: variations in volume, pitch, and quality of voice.

  - Kinesic communication: facial expressions, eye contact, movements, and postures.

  - Proxemic communication: use of interpersonal space.

The medium or setting is not what determines whether shared understandings can be achieved; rather, it is the way you use it and the characteristics of the listeners or audience. The same message may have the potential for rich communication or confusion. Observe how others communicate in this context and determine what approaches they use. Ask questions, ask for feedback, and make an effort to learn about the cultural, professional, or social context.

DO YOU HAVE THE COMMUNICATION SKILLS THAT RESEARCHERS NEED?

There are several communication skills that are essential for researchers. These include:

- Acceptance. You accept feedback.

- Active listening. You pay close attention, focus on the speaker, and avoid distractions like mobile phones.

- Adaptive communication. You adapt your style to your listener.

- Clear communication. You make sure your listener understands the research project and expectations.

- Courtesy. You are polite.

- Emotional intelligence. You display warmth, friendliness, and empathy.

- Being prepared. You review the necessary background information.

- Reflective listening. You check with the speaker to make sure you have understood correctly.

- Generosity with appreciative and constructive feedback. You thank others and give specific feed back when changes are needed.

- Respectfulness of others. You show respect for everyone, whether or not they are of your culture, race, or age group.

- Understanding non-verbal cues. You are attuned to non-verbal messages.

For each of these communication skill sets, ask yourself:

- Who will I need to communicate with on my research project and what do I need to learn to understand their styles and preferences?

- What can I do to improve my verbal communication skills?

- What can I do to improve my non-verbal communication skills?

- What can I do to improve my emotional intelligence? How can I communicate with warmth and empathy?

- What online communication platforms or styles will be best for this project? Do I need to learn new online communication skills that are different from the ones I use with my friends?

- When will synchronous communications (meetings, phone calls, text messaging, video chats, or videoconferencing) be preferable to asynchronous communications (email and posted documents)?

- How can I improve my face-to-face communication skills?

- What boundaries will be crossed in my research project (national, ethnic, organizational culture, or language)? What skills will I need to communicate effectively in this context?

Collaborative researchers can accomplish more together

4

Section

How do I collaborate fearlessly as a co-researcher or co-author?

summary

When you create realistic
agreements and systems of
accountability, you become
the partner with whom others
want to collaborate.

Being able to work with others is essential

Look at research articles on your desktop and books on your shelf. Most of them include more than one author's name. Clearly, being able to work with others is an essential skill set!

Sometimes the scholars collaborated on the writing, drawing on and meshing their work. Other times scholars collaborate on the research and then work together to disseminate findings. Successful collaborative partners realize that attention is needed to the process, as well as to the project at hand. They find that others' expertise and insights enrich their work. Unsuccessful collaborative partners aggravate and disappoint others, who make mental notes to avoid inviting that person to future projects. Think about how you can become the kind of partner others welcome to their projects.

BE THE COLLABORATIVE PARTNER YOU'D WANT ON A PROJECT

Missed deadlines and unresponsive to email. Incomplete or inadequate work. Expectations that others will pick up the missing pieces. These are common complaints about a partner from people whose collaborative projects were unsuccessful. Becoming the kind of partner others want to work with is an important step in becoming a successful researcher.

Not every joint effort is a collaboration. My definition is:

> Collaboration is an interactive process that engages two or more individuals or groups who work together to achieve outcomes they could not accomplish independently. Collaboration is characterized by shared purpose and trust.

Let's look at each part of this definition. The 'interactive process' is at the heart of collaboration. It is the heart of collaboration: give-and-take between partners. We collaborate because partners' contributions are needed to do something that we could not do on our own. We might need specific expertise, perspectives, or simply more people to complete a large-scale project. Sometimes we collaborate to learn from each other, but create our own outcomes. For example, a writing circle could be a very beneficial collaboration, but each writer generates their own final article.

BE
SELF-AWARE

Being a valued partner means accepting that we can accomplish something together that I cannot do on my own. To do so I need to be self-aware about my strengths and have thought through what I can give to this collaborative project. But perhaps more importantly, I need to be self-aware about the limits to my knowledge and skills in order to be receptive to others' input and critiques. If my mindset is 'I could write this article better on my own!' then I am not able to listen and accept the feedback needed to generate the desired outcomes.

We often think about collaboration in terms of a group of people working together. But the group is made up of individuals and essential ingredients for successful collaboration derive from the individuals involved, in particular trust, generosity, and integrity. In order to be a valuable player in the collaborative project, we need to make sense of the project and how we fit.

WHOSE PURPOSE?
WHY ARE WE COLLABORATING?

Collaboration involves working towards a shared purpose. However, the purpose of the project, and of the people assembled to complete it, varies depending on whose idea it was. Did the motivation for the project originate from within the group or from outside the group? If it emerged from group members then there is an intrinsic motivation to succeed. If others assigned or required you to be on the project, if you are there involuntarily, then time will be needed to build commitment to the purpose.

TRUST –
YOU CAN'T
COLLABORATE
WITHOUT IT

We need to be able to trust collaborative partners and be trustworthy members of the group. We can think about two kinds: *personal*, the trust we have in the individuals, and *strategic*, the trust we have in the rules, policies, or parameters associated with the organization or institution. For example, we have personal trust in individuals to be honest, to carry out what we have agreed, and to honour confidentiality. We have strategic trust in a journal to honour their stated mission, to carry out fair and objective peer reviews, and to publish the article in a timely fashion. In a classroom setting, we have personal trust with fellow students on a project and strategic trust in the instructor and institution to guide and assess us fairly.

LEARN TO
COLLABORATE!

Use the tips below to think about how you will improve as a collaborative partner

Tips for successful collaboration

1 Commit to common purpose: Articulate your goals

What do you want to achieve? If we don't know what we want and hope for from our partner(s), how can we expect them to meet our expectations?

2 Reflect on your role

Reflect on the expectations, strengths (and shortcomings) we bring to the group.

3   Plan to collaborate

Schedules and deadlines can make us feel that we should just jump into the project. However, making time to plan and agree to a collaborative process before we start the project can save precious hours in the long run. Two important points should guide this discussion:

- Agree to communicate

    Communication and trust are interrelated: we develop mutual trust when we understand each other. We need to think carefully about how, and how often, to communicate. Will we set checkpoints and hold meetings on a regular basis or just connect on an as-needed basis? When we send an email, what response time do we feel is appropriate? Who will be responsible for communicating with the external stakeholders, editors, etc.?

- Design a work plan

    A work plan establishes who will do what, when, and how. Create a timeline and checkpoints. Clarify roles and the decision-making process you will use.

Get it?

Q: What are three defining elements of collaboration?

A: Interactive process, shared purpose, and trust.

Got it!

I NOW
UNDERSTAND
THE IMPORTANCE
OF SUCCESSFUL
COLLABORATION
AND HOW TO BE A
COLLABORATIVE
PARTNER

#LittleQuickFix

Section

5

Researchers understand the implications of being an insider or an outsider

Why is it important to take a position in relation to my research?

summary

Decisions about the ways your study
works will vary depending or whether
you are an insider or outsider.

It is important to be self-aware and transparent

Sometimes researchers study what they know because they understand the problem from first-hand experience. Other times, researchers discover a gap in the literature that points to a need for new understandings, and study it as an outsider. It is important to be self-aware and transparent about your relationship to the phenomenon, research setting, cultural context, and other elements of the study. Whichever option fits the study, researchers should strive to be curious and open-minded, as we considered in Section 2. Being honest about our position enhances our credibility as researchers.

When designing and conducting research you typically focus on the research problem, methodology, and methods. Keep in mind that as a researcher, you are inherently part of the research. The researcher should know from the earliest design stage where he or she stands to guard against biases or conflicts of interest. It is essential to be self-aware and transparent about your position.

AS A RESEARCHER, YOU ARE INHERENTLY PART OF THE RESEARCH

Two terms are commonly used to describe the roles of insiders and outsiders in a research context. The term 'emic' refers to an insider. The term 'etic' refers to an outsider. There are, of course, degrees of relationship. Given that the situation is not always black and white, you could think of the options as a continuum, rather than either/or. The options are not choices between good and bad – insider and outsider research can both be empirically sound. The choice should be appropriate to the purpose of the study.

In an etic study, the researcher is on the outside looking in. The researcher aims to remove themselves and eliminate biases from data and its collection. The researcher defines a research problem based on a gap in the literature. Instruments are reviewed and tested prior to the study to reduce researcher influence.

ETIC
STUDIES

At the next point on the continuum, the researcher is familiar with the culture, community, or setting or has experienced the research problem. Next, moving in the direction of an emic study, the researcher shares characteristics with the population being investigated, but is not a member of the group. To some extent we are all in this grey area when we conduct research about problems we care about within our own field of study, culture, or social environment.

In an emic study, the researcher draws the research problem and questions from experience or their own history. The motivation for conducting the study is based on the researcher's personal connection to the phenomenon or participants being investigated. The emic researcher sees a problem in their personal or professional lives, organizations or communities, country or society. They didn't need to read scholarly literature to know this problem exists and why it is important to study. They want to understand it so we can generate findings that might help. In this situation, their position is one of an insider.

EMIC STUDIES

Some methodologies are inherently oriented to an insider or outsider research role. Researchers are necessarily insiders when they conduct autoethnographies, participant observations, or action research. Some insiders contribute data in the form of reflective journal entries or field notes to complement data collected from participants. Researchers are typically outsiders when they conduct research using surveys, observations, or archival or historical record analysis. You might think that when using quantitative methods or Big Data, you are immune from the need to consider your position vis-à-vis the study. However, you might have insider perspectives that would influence your choices and the ways you interpret results.

Insider status may help the researcher gain access to a research site or participants. An insider who has commonalities with participants might be able to develop trust and rapport more quickly. At the same time, the outsider can bring broader, objective understandings of the research problem into the study and devise thought-provoking or challenging interview questions. Whether inside, outside, or somewhere in the middle, the researcher needs to state a clear position and provide a rationale for how that position serves the study.

ALWAYS STATE YOUR POSITION

Consider these questions when you are reflecting on your insider or outsider position in relation to your research:

- Am I motivated to study questions or problems related to my own experiences or phenomena I have personally observed? Or, am I motivated to study questions or problems I have not personally experienced?

- How might insider status help or harm my study?

- How close is too close?

- At what point does the degree of intimacy with the organization, group, or participant, or familiarity with the research problem, jeopardize the researcher's ability to carry out the study?

- When do conflicts of interest and/or researcher bias taint the findings?

Get it?

Q: What terms are used to describe a researcher's relationship to the study?

A: Emic positions are insiders; etic positions are outsiders.

Got it!

Stay focused and make time for self-care

How can I achieve my goal as a respected researcher?

A

summary

Stay true to your intentions by building a supportive network, reflective and mindful practices, and systems of accountability.

Find ways to ensure you remain true to your intentions

Time pressures, distractions, and competing priorities make it hard to stay true to your intentions. Like-minded researchers, whether peers or mentors, can encourage you to stay on track. Friends and partners not associated with the research can offer needed moral support (and a timely cup of tea). Still, it's important that motivation and commitment comes from you first and foremost. Finding ways to reflect will help. A sustainable system of checkpoints and accountability is essential.

FIND THE BEST STRATEGIES FOR YOU

Research is complex and time-consuming. For many researchers, it is one activity among many. Being able to focus solely on one's research without other academic, professional, and family responsibilities is a luxury. Most researchers must learn to juggle to-do lists and schedules. However, some things are not 'juggleable'! We can't de-prioritize the need to act from a place of impeccable character and utmost integrity. We can't say, 'I'll fit in being ethical next week.' We can't step away from partners with whom we need to communicate or collaborate.

Here are four strategies to try:

1 Build your research support network. When you are a student, you take for granted the presence of peers who are all engaged in the same assignments. You take for granted that you have faculty, advisors, and others you can go to with questions. You can develop these kinds of networks to help you stay true to yourself, your research, and publication goals by joining professional societies and associations in your field and looking for opportunities to get involved. Some societies have local chapters with face-to-face meetings. Take advantage of such meetings to find like-minded people who would appreciate mutual support.

Ask two or three others to join you in an informal group (which can be virtual). Make sure that you include time to discuss your personal development goals as well as your professional ones. Finding a mentor who wants to support your efforts can be challenging, but don't be afraid to ask.

2 Reflect on your experiences and insights. In addition to discussions with peers and mentors, make time to reflect. Start a research journal (analogue or digital) to record your questions and insights.

3 Be mindful. Mindfulness means paying attention to the moment. This kind of focused awareness can help you get through times when projects seem so big and goals so unattainable. Stop mentally racing ahead and be present with what you are doing, even if it seems like a small step. By taking a more accepting, nonjudgmental approach, you can avoid the kind of self-doubt that is ultimately self-defeating.

4   Create and honour a system of accountability for research goals and for character. You have already accomplished goals – how did you do it? What works for one person does not work for another. Checklists and checkpoints, timelines, and calendar notations help some and not others. You might use a whiteboard on the wall or prefer an app on your mobile phone. What works for you? It doesn't matter what kind of system you use, just pick one!

Throughout this book you have been introduced to both practical and aspirational aspects of a researcher's role. Are you ready to commit to becoming the scholar others look to as an example of integrity, trustworthiness, responsiveness, and responsibility – in addition to the value you add with your research findings?

DEVELOP YOUR OWN STRATEGIES

Which strategies are right for me?

☐ Build my research support network

☐ Reflect on my experiences and insights

☐ Be mindful

☐ Create and honour a system of accountability for research goals and for character

Do I have ideas about how to make them work for me?

Yes, they are:

. . . .

. . . .

. . . .

. . . .

Not yet, I will need to take these steps in order to make a plan:

. . . .

. . . .

. . . .

. . . .

What or who will I need to make them work?

☐ People I know and can ask for support and encouragement

☐ People I hope to meet by intentionally building a network

☐ Systems I've used successfully and can adapt for this purpose

☐ Systems I need to develop, starting with:

. . . .

. . . .

. . . .

. . . .

Research activities can take us to places that are different from our social or cultural worlds where we are comfortable. We might find that the people we interact with have limited use of the language we use, are resistant to answering our questions, or that they are more comfortable showing, rather than telling, what they think or feel. Practise other styles so when you face such a situation, you have alternatives to try.

Ask a friend to role play and help you practise communication skills. Practise with a non-threatening decision, such as what movie to see or where to have lunch.

1. First, state your own strong preference, then ask the other person for theirs. Second, on a different topic, ask your friend for their preference, then voice your own.

2. Describe options using pictures (drawings or photographs) instead of words.

3. Communicate a message where your words are at odds with negative non-verbal cues.

4. Communicate the same message verbally, making eye contact and smiling, and then in writing.

Discuss your friend's responses to each style. Which engendered trust and which made your friend feel you were being negative?

Draw this starting point and add your strategies.
Hang it on your wall or post it to your desktop!

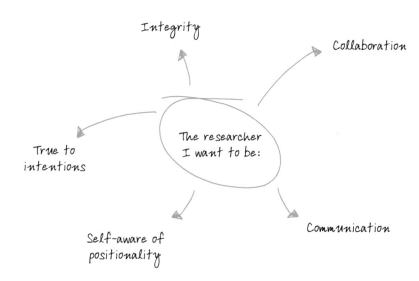

Open a new document or choose a paper journal that appeals to you. Create headings for each area of researcher character and identity you want to be able to exemplify. Take a few moments to add something each day, even if it is only a few words or a doodle. Use your journal to collect and save:

- notes from supportive friends or your mentor

- inspiring poems or essays

- images or drawings

- citations and excerpts from articles or studies about researchers' roles and practices.

I CAN NOW FEEL
CONFIDENT THAT
I CAN DO MORE
THAN CONDUCT
RESEARCH, I CAN BE
A *RESEARCHER!*

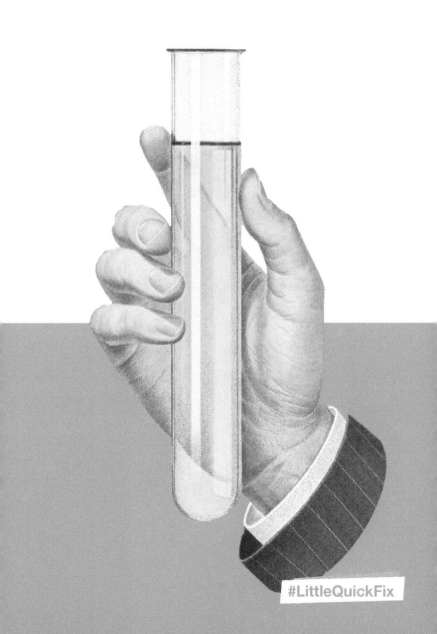
#LittleQuickFix

To ensure that you have mastered the essentials involved in studying theories and can use them in your own future research, work through the questions in this checklist

Can you:

☐ Identify ways that you will act with integrity throughout the research process? If not, revisit Section 1.

☐ Feed your curiosity for exploring with an open mind? If not, revisit Section 2.

☐ Approach new situations and readings with critical and creative thinking? If not, revisit Section 2.

☐ Assess communication needs for the projects you are in and be a responsive communicator? If not, revisit Section 3.

HOW TO KNOW
YOU
ARE
DONE

☐ Listen respectfully to others, even when you don't agree with them? If not, revisit Section 3.

☐ Take the steps that are necessary to ensure that collaboration is successful? If not, revisit Section 4.

☐ Be self-aware about your position as an insider or outsider and address any potential biases? If not, revisit Section 5.

☐ Approach your work as a mindful researcher who is attentive to the moment, rather than being distressed by the time and steps needed to complete large research projects? If not, revisit Section 6.

☐ Make time to reflect on each step along the way, and the development of your character as a credible scholar? If not, revisit Section 6.

Glossary

Asynchronous communications Not present at the same time, with a gap between the message and response. It is common in written or electronic communications, such as email or posted documents.

Autoethnographies Studies conducted by researchers that involve reflecting on and analysing their own experiences, and finding larger meanings in social or cultural contexts.

Collaboration It is an interactive process that engages two or more individuals or groups who work together to achieve outcomes they could not accomplish independently. Collaboration is characterized by shared purpose and trust.

Creative thinking Refers to processes that involve the use of the imagination or original ideas to produce something unique.

Critical thinking Refers to processes that involve objective analysis and evaluation of an issue or resource materials.

Field or discipline A broad area of study related to academic or professional practice. For example, education can be described as a field or discipline. Professors, teachers, and others are practitioners who work in this field.

Methodology Approaches used to design and conduct research. The methodology describes how the design links the choice of methods to the research problem and purpose of the study.

Mindfulness Being aware and in the present moment.

Research design Blueprint for a proposed study that aligns the epistemological position, theory, methodology, methods, and ethical issues in a plan to study a defined research problem.

Synchronous communications Present at the same time, able to respond without a lag in time, either face-to-face or electronically.